BRAVE LADIES

WHO CHANGED THE WORLD
coloring book

A Feminist Celebration of Courageous Women

VOLUME 1

WRITTEN AND ILLUSTRATED BY

KAELEE JENSEN

Little REBEL ROSIE

Printed in the United States of America

Who was Amelia Earhart?

1897-1937

Amelia was a Daredevil.

Raised by the first woman to successfully summit Pike's Peak, Amelia's mother did not discourage her fearless tendencies. As a kid Amelia raced sleds downhill in the winter, climbed trees in the summer, and got pretty good at shooting a gun while hunting rats in the woods behind her house for target practice. All hobbies that were considered too wild and unladylike for a young girl. Amelia didn't care!

When she was a young woman she served as a military nurse in Toronto, held a difficult job driving trucks across the country, and almost died from the Spanish Flu.

At age 23 Amelia experienced a short flight as a passenger on a small plane, and from that point on flying was her passion. Amelia worked long hours at many different jobs to pay for her flying lessons and to purchase her first airplane.

The gutsy and determined Amelia learned all kinds of stunts and performed at air shows. She was the first woman to reach an altitude of 14,000 feet, setting a world record. She became the first female passenger on a flight across the Atlantic Ocean when she navigated the trip with another pilot. That wasn't enough for Amelia, she had to complete the flight herself. She became the first woman to pilot a solo trip across the same ocean.

Between 1930 and 1935 Amelia set seven speed and distance records for women. She insisted she could do anything a man could, and Amelia lectured around the country to encourage women to attend college. Amelia also started a commercial airline, and founded a club for female aviators called the Ninety-Nines, a group that went on to ferry planes during WWII as the renowned Women Airforce Service Pilots (WASP).

Amelia was a bold, audacious woman who took on any challenge, and never let anyone tell her what to do - or what not to do.

The 1937 disappearance of Amelia, her navigator Fred Noonan, and their airplane while circumnavigating the globe is a mystery that has never been solved.

"What you do makes a difference, and you have to decide what kind of difference you want to make."

Who is Jane Goodall?

1934-

Jane is an advocate for the voiceless.

From a very young age Jane was fascinated by animals. Inspired by the book Doctor Doolittle, Jane dreamt of Africa. She worked tirelessly to make her dream a reality. When she was only twenty-two, Jane boarded a boat and sailed across the sea, arriving in Kenya on her twenty-third birthday. While there she met the anthropologist Louis Leakey, who hired her as a secratary. Dr. Leakey soon realized Jane's talents, and he sent Jane to study chimpanzees in Tanzania. Jane's work in the years she spent living in a tent in the wilderness of Africa, would change the world forever. The curious but patient Jane gradually earned the trust of the chimpanzees and was able to observe their behavior in a way no one ever had in the past.

Jane was steadfast in her observations. She discovered how very similar chimpanzees are to humans - in their use of tools, their social interaction, and the way they nurture their families. She established that chimpanzees have far more knowledge than previously believed, and that chimpanzees display a wide range of complex emotions that were once thought to be uniquely human.

Jane became well-known for her revolutionary discoveries, and was accepted into the doctoral program at Cambridge without an undergraduate degree. Jane encountered criticism at Cambridge for the way she humanized the chimpanzees, but she refused to bow to pressure.

Jane is a conservationist and animal rights activist who has been honored with many awards. She founded the Jane Goodall Institute, which protects great apes and their habitat while promoting sustainability and conservation. She also established the Roots and Shoots program to educate young people about conservation, animal rights, and caring for the planet that we all share. Jane will always be known as a pioneer in the research of chimpanzees in the wild, and a protector of the lands that they inhabit. Jane continues to travel over 300 days a year, spreading her message worldwide.

Who were the Suffragettes?

The word "Suffragette" was first used to describe women campaigning for the right to vote in an article in a British newspaper in 1906. Suffragettes in Britain were jailed for their protests, abused, and torturously force fed when they went on hunger strikes. One Suffragette even threw herself beneath the King's horse in an act of protest, resulting in her death. The British suffragettes raised the profile of the issue of women's votes to that of national consideration, and after World War I, in 1918, the Representation of the People Act was passed by Parliament giving some, but not all women in the United Kingdom the right to vote.

In America during the 1850s, the women's rights movement gathered steam, but lost momentum when the Civil War began. Almost immediately after the war ended, the 14th and 15th Amendments to the Constitution raised familiar questions of suffrage and citizenship. Starting in 1910, some states in the West began to extend the vote to women for the first time in almost 20 years. (Idaho and Utah had given women the right to vote at the end of the 19th century.)

World War I slowed the suffragists' campaign, but women's work on behalf of the war effort was undeniable evidence that they were just as patriotic and deserving of full citizenship as men, which helped them advance their argument. In 1920 the 19th Amendment to the Constitution was finally ratified, granting women the right to vote.

Womens suffrage is a battle that has been fought worldwide, and while many women in the world today do have the right to vote, the fight for equality rages onward in so many places.

A few of the many notable Suffragettes:

United Kingdom: Emmeline Pankhurst and her daughters Sylvia and Christabel Pankhurst, Emily Wilding Davison, Millicent Fawcett, Elizabeth Garrett Anderson, Lydia Becker, & Helen Taylor.

United States: Susan B. Anthony, Sojourner Truth, Ida B. Wells, Elizabeth Cady Stanton, Louisa May Alcott, Alice Paul, Dorothy Day, Amelia Bloomer, Jeannette Rankin, Lucy Stone, & Matilda Joslyn Gage

Who was Josephine Baker?

1906-1975

Josephine was radical.

It is difficult to contain the fantastic life of the bold & brave performer Josephine Baker on one small page. She spent her youth in poverty before learning to dance and leaving her first husband to find success on Broadway. Initially she was turned away. Josephine learned all of the dances anyway, and as soon as a dancer quit, Josephine was hired. She stole the show by acting clumsy and goofy on purpose, and gained popularity among audiences quickly. She was offered a job in Paris, and decided to try it out due to the rejection she faced in America as a woman of color.

Josephine Baker danced her way onto a Paris stage and right into the hearts of the French, who were fascinated by her comedic performances, and controversial costumes. Josephine quickly became the highest paid performer in Paris. She felt liberated in France. While her reputation thrived in Paris, upon returning to America to perform it was evident that nothing had changed. The critics and audiences were hostile towards her, and she returned to Paris heartbroken. White audiences could not accept a black woman of style, grace, and sophistication. Josephine chose to become a French citizen not long after the disappointing experience.

She worked as a spy for the French Resistance during World War II. She used her fame to her advantage traveling the world for parties and events, and collecting information in secret. She would write messages on her sheet music in invisible ink and pin confidential photos to her underwear, betting that due to her fame she would not be strip-searched.

Jospehine adopted and raised many children of different ethnicities, to prove to the world that we could all live peacefully and happily together. She called them her Rainbow Tribe.

She was very involved in the the Civil Rights movement in America, and always refused to perform for segregated audiences while touring. Josephine devoted herself to fighting the segregation and racism she had experienced, and was invited to speak by Martin Luther King Jr, alongside Rosa Parks. Josephine did return to the United States for a performance at Carnegie Hall, and was met with a standing ovation before she even performed. Josephine was so moved by her reception that she wept openly on stage.

Josephine performed at the 50th anniversary celebration of her Paris debut in front of an adoring crowd full of prominent and progressive people. She passed away a few days later. Her funeral was attended by thousands, and she is the only American-born woman to receive full French military honors at her funeral. She was a great lover of life and humanity and devoted herself to making the world a more hospitable place and securing a better future for its citizens.

Josephine Baker

"Surely the day will
come when color means
nothing more
than the skin tone,
when religion
is seen uniquely
as a way to speak
one's soul; when birth
places have the
weight of a throw
of the dice
and all men are
born free...."

Who was Joan of Arc?

1412-1431

As a young woman with strong religious and patriotic conviction, Joan of Arc dedicated herself to relieving oppression.

At the age of 13, Joan began to hear voices, which she determined had been sent by God to give her a mission of overwhelming importance: to save France by expelling its enemies, and to install Prince Charles as its rightful King.

The clever Joan convinced Prince Charles that she would not rest until he was crowned, and the Prince awarded Joan an army. At the age of 18 Joan led the army to Orléans, then under siege from the English. After sending off a defiant letter to the enemy, Joan led several successful French assaults against them, forcing them to retreat. Prince Charles was crowned King.

Her miraculous victory made the young woman famous, but she was captured not long after by the enemy. She was tried on numerous counts including witchcraft, heresy, and dressing like a man. In order to distance himself from her perceived fanaticism, Prince Charles did not attempt to negotiate her release. For a moment Joan faltered, signing a confession that she had never received divine guidance, however she soon recanted her confession, donned men's clothing, and she was charged, tried, and burned at the stake.

Her fame only increased after her death, and 20 years later a new trial ordered by Charles VII cleared her name. She has been named the Patron Saint of France, and has inspired numerous works of art and literature through out the centuries. In 1920 she was canonized by Pope Benedict XV.

"If we want scientists and engineers in the future we should be cultivating the girls as much as the boys."

Who Was Sally Ride?

1951-2012

Sally Ride was the first American woman to fly in space.

Sally grew up in California where she attended Stanford University, earning a degree in physics. She was interested in science from an early age, despite it being an unpopular subject for a girl to study. Sally was a college student at the time that NASA began looking for female astronauts in 1977. She saw an ad in the school newspaper inviting women to apply to the astronaut program, and she applied immediately. She was one of six women chosen! On June 18, 1983 Sally became the first American female astronaut to launch into spaces as she took her trailblazing first ride aboard the space shuttle Challenger. Her job was to work the robotic arm, which she used to help put satellites into space. She then flew on the space shuttle Challenger again in 1984.

As a woman Sally dealt with ridiculous and sexist questions from the media about her makeup routine, how she would handle feminine hygiene, the bathroom facilities in space, and whether she cried during training. Male astronauts were never asked these kinds of questions.

After her space shuttle missions, Sally began teaching at the University of California in San Diego. Sally was trying to find ways to encourage women and girls who wanted to study science and math, when she came up with the idea for NASA's EarthKAM project. EarthKAM lets middle school students take pictures of Earth using a camera on the International Space Station, and then study the pictures.

In 2003 Sally was added to the Astronaut Hall of Fame, which honors astronauts for their hard work. Until her death on July 23, 2012, Ride continued to encourage students - especially girls - to study science and mathematics, and pursue careers in those fields. She wrote learning materials for students and teachers, and worked with science programs and festivals around the United States. After her death it was revealed in her obituary that Sally was not only the first American woman to fly in space, but Sally was also the first gay astronaut to fly in space. She had a loving relationship with her female partner for 27 years.

No one had ever heard
of a black woman pilot in
1919. I refused to take
no for an answer"

Who Was Bessie Coleman?

1892-1926

Bessie Coleman was born in Texas in 1892. Her mother was African American, and her father had both African American and Native American heritage. Bessie worked hard for her education, and started college, but she ran out of money after only one semester and returned home to work. She soon moved to Chicago to live with her brothers, and attended beauty school so she could earn a decent living.

While working in Chicago she became interested in flying. Due to the racist and sexist attitudes of the time, Bessie would not be accepted into an American flying school as a black woman. She would have to go to France to learn to fly. She worked hard as a manicurist and managed a restaurant, while also taking French lessons. When Bessie had finally saved up enough money she traveled to France where she attended the Fédération Aéronautique Internationale. She was the first woman of either African American, or Native American descent to earn an Aviation Pilot's License. She returned to America, and began performing dangerous stunts at air shows for large crowds, because it was the only way to make money as a pilot.

"Queen Bess," as she was known, was a highly popular draw. Invited to important events and often interviewed by newspapers, she was admired by many. Bessie traveled the country, refusing to fly for audiences where black people would not be allowed. Bessie was very passionate about desegregating aviation. She said you had never really lived until you had flown, and that the air was the only place free from prejudices. She dreamed of opening a flight school for black students.

At one point Bessie crashed her plane, resulting in serious injuries. She wouldn't let the injuries stop her from doing what she loved, and swore she would fly again as soon as she was healed. And she did! Later, when she was only 34, she fell from a plane during a test flight, and was killed.

"Were there none who were discontented with what they have, the world would never reach anything better."

Who Was Florence Nightingale?

1820-1910

Florence Revolutionized the Nursing industry.

Born at a time when middle-class women in Europe were expected to marry and raise a family, Florence sensed a calling from an early age, and believed she was destined for something greater. She was particularly gifted in academics as a child, and had a strong sense of moral duty to help the poor. She became interested in nursing, but due to her parents' insistence, Florence put off her formal study. Instead she privately studied any information she could on health and hospitals. After a courtship of nine years Florence rejected her suitor, and persuaded her family to allow her to pursue her career. She traveled to Dusseldorf and completed three months of nurse training. Upon returning to London she was quickly given a position as a superintendent of a hospital.

During the Crimean War, reports flooded in about the dreadful conditions and lack of medical supplies suffered by injured soldiers. Florence gathered and trained a group of 38 nurses, who traveled with her to Turkey to organize and improve the conditions of the hospital. She became known as the Lady of the Lamp for her ritual of checking on the wounded and sick throughout the night by lamplight. She implemented revolutionary reforms that included daily washing of bedding, changing of dressings, and consistent hand-washing. She also insisted that healthy food, plenty of clean water, and fresh air were essential for healing.

Florence was a pioneer in the use of statistical methods to design hospitals and programs to maximize healthcare. She used advanced visual charts to explain that many were dying not of their injuries, but from the spread of bacteria and disease due to the filthy conditions and lack of proper sanitation within the hospitals. In light of Florence's work, new army medical, sanitary science, and statistics departments were established to improve healthcare. Florence published books on nursing, and a nursing school was founded in her name.

Florence Nightingale's work was instrumental in establishing nursing as a respectable career for women, and transformed hospitals into clean and healthy spaces for treatment and recovery.

"A feminist is anyone who recognizes
the equality and full humanity of women and men."

Who is Gloria Steinem?

1934-

Credited as a leader of Second Wave Feminism, Gloria Steinem believed that discrimination based on gender, race, class, age, or ethnicity were all human and civil rights violations, and they needed to be confronted together, instead of as separate issues.

Gloria was a writer, organizer and activist, who confronted the cultural beliefs of the time about women's roles in families and society. She graduated from Smith College, and was selected for a two year fellowship in India. Steinem's experience in India made her aware of the extent of human suffering in the world, and the privilege she had experienced growing up in America. She returned to the US with a strong sense of social justice, determined to make a difference. Beginning work as a freelance journalist, she became deeply involved in the political movements that were stirring thousands of her generation into action. Her quick wit, good sense of humor, and fiery comebacks gained media attention, and she was able to shine a more positive light on the feminist movement than other feminist leaders during the time, making feminism more mainstream.

Some of the accomplishments of the Second Wave of Feminism include:
-Women gaining control over when they choose to have children, giving them more time to pursue a college education and a career.
-Employers being prohibited from hiring only men, and other types of gender discrimination in the workplace. This resulted in more opportunities for women within professions that had previously been dominated by men.
-Laws were passed making domestic abuse illegal, and making it easier for women to obtain a divorce.
-A more widespread and accepted belief that women should have autonomy and freedom over their choices, as well as equal rights with men.

Who is Malala Yousafzai?

1997-

Malala Yousafzai, a native of Pakistan, began speaking out at the young age of 11 about the rights of women and girls to gain an education. In Pakistan at the time education was being threatened by the terrorist organization called the Taliban, and Malala risked her life by beginning a blog under a pseudonym, a made-up name, to protect her identity.

In 2011 she was awarded Pakistan's first National Youth Peace Prize. Her popularity angered Taliban leaders, who voted that she should be killed despite their usual rules to spare children. In October of 2012 she was shot in the head on her way home from school, but Malala survived the attack. She is now the youngest ever recipient of a Nobel Peace Prize, which she received at age 17. She co-founded the Malala Fund with her father, to bring awareness to the social and economic impact of girls' education and to empower girls to raise their voices, to unlock their potential and to demand change.

She is a persistent, daring, and outspoken activist, surprising President Obama during their initial meeting at the White house by confronting him about some of the US Military's tactics, and how they might contribute to the rise of terrorist organizations. Malala does not believe that you can stop violence with more violence. She continues to travel the world, raising money to build schools, and spread awareness about the importance of education in attaining peace.

"Extremists have shown
what frightens them most:
a girl with a book"

Malala Yousafzai

Who is Ruth Bader Ginsburg?

1933-

The Notorious Ruth Bader Ginsburg, the tiny and fierce Jewish grandmother, has been ruling on the Supreme Court bench since 1993, and arguing cases in courtrooms for decades prior. She is a devoted advocate of equal rights for women, and is well know for her passionate and witty dissents. In the words of former President Bill Clinton, who nominated her to the Supreme Court, "Ruth Bader Ginsburg cannot be called a liberal or a conservative; she has proved herself too thoughtful for such labels."

She maintained the top spot in her classes at Cornell, Harvard, and Columbia as one of a very small number of women at all three universities. After graduation, she was rejected by every law firm she applied to simply because she was a woman. As a law professor she had to fight for equal pay. She was experiencing first-hand the blatant gender-based discrimination that was negatively impacting the lives of women across the country, and she wanted to do something about it.

As a co-founder of the Womens Rights Project of the ACLU, she argued many landmark cases of gender-discrimination before the Supreme Court, including one where a man was discriminated against. These cases resulted in the establishment of gender as a category of illegal discrimination under Civil Rights legislation, followed by the changing of laws around the country in favor of equal rights.

Ginsburg was only the second woman to hold a position on the Supreme Court, the first being Sandra Day O'Connor. After O'Connor retired in 2006, Ginsburg was the only woman on the 9 member court until President Barack Obama nominated Sonia Sotomayor and Elena Kagan as associate justices in 2009 and 2010.

Ruth Bader Ginsburg has recently become an unlikely pop-culture icon, as a Supreme Court Justice in her eighties, who is well known and well loved by a new generation of politically active liberal young people.

"Energy rightly applied and directed will accomplish anything"

Who was Nellie Bly?

1864-1922

Before she was known as the adventurous and daring Nellie Bly, Elizabeth Jane Cochran was a young woman who was forced to abandon her academic studies in order to support her family. She and her mother were running a boarding house, when an article appeared in their local paper stating that women belonged in the home, cooking, cleaning, and raising children. She crafted a fiery rebuttal, submitted it to *The Pittsburg Dispatch*, and the impressive piece landed her a job. While there she took on her pen name, and wrote for $5 a week.

She soon moved to New York to write for *New York World*, where she posed as a mental patient and was admitted to an asylum for 10 days. The infamous exposé on the mistreatment of mental patients resulted in a large-scale investigation and much needed improvements in healthcare.

{ "The insane asylum on Blackwell's Island is a human rat-trap. It is easy to get in, but once there it is impossible to get out." }

The piece was later published into a book entitled Ten Days in a Mad-House.

Bly went on to gain more fame when she lobbied the *New York World* to sponsor her on a trip around the world, inspired by the Jules Verne novel Around the World in 80 Days. The paper's business manager commented that it would be better to send a man because he would not need a chaperone or as much luggage.
Bly shot back: "Very well. Start the man and I'll start the same day for some other newspaper and beat him." She got the assignment. Bly traveled with only a 16"x7" leather handbag, a hat, and a coat. She traveled by ship, horse, rickshaw, sampan, and burro, and more. The trip was completed in 72 days, 6 hours, 11 minutes and 14 seconds. A world record! Bly later published a book about the experience: Around the World in 72 Days.

Bly was a constant champion of the poor, underprivileged, and underrepresented. She fought to expose violations of human rights and corruption, as well as fighting a constant battle for the rights of working women.

Harriet Tubman

"Every great dream begins
with a dreamer. Always
remember, you have
within you the strength,
the patience, and the
passion to reach
for the stars to change
the world."

Who was Harriet Tubman?

1822-1913

An African American born into slavery, Harriet Tubman suffered several acts of violence during her childhood, resulting in lifelong seizures and headaches. Harriet had a defiant nature, and yearned for freedom. When she was about 27 she escaped from slavery in Maryland, sneaking across the border into Pennsylvania. Harriet bravely returned to Maryland many times, smuggling slaves to freedom through a secret network of abolitionists called the Underground Railroad. They hid runaways, and ensured their safe passage from one safe-house to the next in the dark of night, through swamps, forests, and sometimes hidden in wagons.

Soon laws were passed mandating that escaped slaves living freely in the North could be re-captured and delivered to their former owners in the South, so Tubman re-routed the Underground Railroad to Canada where slavery was outlawed all-together.

Harriet continued to return to Maryland to rescue slaves and deliver them to freedom, rescuing most of her family and many others.

During the American Civil War, Tubman began working for the Union Army as a cook and nurse, and then she became an armed scout and spy. She was the first woman to lead an armed expedition in the war, when she guided the Combahee River Raid, which liberated more than 700 slaves in South Carolina.

Harriet purchased land in New York where she made a large home for her family to live in freedom. She devoted the rest of her life to fighting for civil rights, caring for the welfare of her family and loved ones, and supporting suffrage. She established a care center for elderly African Americans, where she eventually resided Recently the US government unveiled plans to replace Andrew Jackson on the twenty-dollar bill with the face of Harriet Tubman.

Who was Rosie the Riveter?

During World War II the able bodied men in America answered the call to defend our country and many were deployed. Their absence left a gaping hole in the workforce, and Rosie the Riveter represents the many women who took jobs in industrial factories in order to support the war effort.

The iconic image of a woman in coveralls and a red bandana with white polka dots, clenching her fist, saying, "We can do it!", originated as an advertising campaign by the US government to recruit women into the aviation and munitions industries.

Though women who entered the workforce during World War II were crucial to the war effort, their pay lagged far behind their male counterparts. Female workers rarely earned more than 50 percent of male wages. Women of color earned even less, and took on the less favorable jobs.

In addition to factory work and other home front jobs, some 350,000 women joined the Armed Services, serving at home and abroad.

During the war, Rosie the Riveter became the most famous representation of working women. While the need for Rosie propaganda ceased after the war, her we-can-do-it attitude has left an imprint in history. The number of women in the workforce never did fall back to pre-wartime levels. The result was the beginning of a change in attitudes towards gender roles. Today Rosie the Riveter has been adopted as a confident feminist icon, empowering us to be strong, capable, independant, brave women.

"We can do it!"

Who was Maya Angelou?

1928-2014

The always eloquent Maya Angelou was a performer, writer, poet, and activist. Named Marguerite Annie Johnson, her brother Bailey gave her the nick-name Maya.

At only seven, Maya experienced a trauma, and stopped speaking for many years. A woman she admired encouraged the silent child to read everything she could, and she learned to love poetry, which eventually led Maya to rediscover her voice.

Maya won a scholarship as a teenager to a performing arts school in the Bay Area, but dropped out of school at 14 to become San Francisco's very first female cable car conductor. She gave birth to her only son, Guy, at age 17. She raised and supported him herself.

She spent the 50's performing on the stage, and the 60s living abroad in Egypt and Ghana. Angelou was an active Civil Rights supporter for her entire life, working with the remarkable Malcom X, and Martin Luther King Jr. Her work is viewed as a defense of Black Culture

She is most famous for her memoir I Know Why the Caged Bird Sings and the poem that she recited at President Bill Clinton's Inauguration entitled, On the Pulse of Morning, which earned her a Grammy Award. There have been attempts to ban some of her books from libraries within the US.

During her life Maya was awarded many honors, the highest of which was the Presidential Medal of Freedom; awarded by President Barack Obama. Angelou never did attend college, but was awarded over 50 honorary degrees. She taught as a professor for a time, and continued to lecture regularly well into her eighties.

"I am a Woman
Phenomenally.
Phenomenal Woman,
that's me."

-*Phenomenal Woman* (poem)

Who was Marie Curie?

1867-1934

Madame Marie Curie is history's most illustrious female scientist. Known from a young age to have a prodigious memory, she won awards throughout grade-school for her fantastic academic performance, but had to begin working soon after to support herself.

Marie and her sister both wished to go to college, but it was not allowed for women in Poland, where they were born and raised. The devoted sisters took turns paying for each other's education in France. Marie funded her sister's medical studies, and then she attended the Sorbonne University, earning her PhD in Physics.

Curie and her associates (including her husband Pierre) discovered and studied new elements, naming them Polonium and Radium. They coined the term "radioactive" to describe the elements they had discovered, because the elements put off rays of energy. Together they were awarded a Nobel Prize in physics, making Marie the first woman to win the prize. She later became the only woman to earn the Nobel Prize in more than one category when she was awarded another in the field of Chemistry.

Marie realized the usefulness of x-rays in medicine, and created small x-ray machines that could be transported by truck, helping doctors immensely in treating wounded soldiers during World War I.

The birth of her two daughters, Irène and Ève, in 1897 and 1904 did not interrupt Marie's intensive scientific work.

Marie achieved another first for women, as the first female professor of Physics at the Sorbonne University. She worked tirelessly in the field of science, making new discoveries that changed the world. Her work has resulted in the discovery of many treatments for cancer.

Marie herself died of cancer, due to the many years of exposure to radioactive materials she experienced while doing research.

"Be less curious about people and more curious about ideas."

Thank you!

🌐 LITTLEREBELROSIE.COM

✉ LITTLEREBELROSIE@GMAIL.COM

Etsy ETSY.COM/SHOP/LITTLEREBELROSIE

📷 @LITTLEREBELROSIE

LOOK FOR US ON AMAZON